The Interior Landscape

This book is one of the volumes sponsored by the Asian Literature Program of the Asia Society, Inc.

UNESCO COLLECTION OF REPRESENTATIVE WORKS

INDIAN SERIES

This book has been accepted in the Indian Translations Series of the United Nations Educational, Scientific, and Cultural Organization

(UNESCO)

The Interior Landscape

LOVE POEMS FROM A
CLASSICAL TAMIL ANTHOLOGY

TRANSLATED BY

A. K. Ramanujan

Indiana University Press
BLOOMINGTON AND LONDON

First Midland Book Edition 1975

Published in Canada by Fitzhenry & Whiteside Limited, Don Mills, Ontario

Library of Congress catalog card number: 67-25136
ISBN: 0-253-20185-3 pa

Manufactured in the United States of America

For my mother

CONTENTS

Translator's Note

The poems in this book were selected from the *Kuṟun-tokai,* one of the eight anthologies of classical Tamil ascribed to the first three centuries A.D.

The translations and the afterword (which some readers may prefer to read first) are two parts of one effort. The effort is to try and make a non-Tamil reader experience in English something of what a native experiences when he reads classical Tamil poems. Anyone translating a poem into a foreign language is, at the same time, trying to *translate* a foreign reader into a native one.

The originals would not speak freely through the translations to present-day readers if the renderings were not in modern English, and if they were not poems themselves in some sense. By the same token, the translations had to be close, as close as my sense of English and Tamil would allow.

My fidelity has been chiefly to the structure of the poems. This concern has led me away from translating every poem line by line. Rather I have rendered a poem phrase by phrase as each phrase articulates the total poem. I have paid special attention to the images and their placement. Sometimes I have made explicit typographic approximations to what I thought was the inner form of the poem; broken up lines and arranged them in little blocks and paragraphs, or arranged them step-wise; I have tried to suggest by the spacing the distance or the closeness of elements in the original syntax. The Tamil poets had no capitals, punctuation marks, nor any regular end-rhymes in the kind of blank verse they used for all these poems. Tamil, unlike English, has a "free word-order". The poets make excellent use of this freedom to create their poetic forms; the central nuance of a poem is most often enacted by the unusual yet perfectly acceptable positioning of sentence-parts and by the strategic placing of 'insets' of imagery. The formal aspects of Tamil poetry are discussed in the Afterword. So I will not go into any details here. I only request that the reader look upon the visual shape of the poems as nothing arbitrary or eccentric but as a way of indicating the design of the original poems. They are an essential part of the effort at fidelity. In this effort, a dense adjective-packed, participle-crowded Tamil poem of four lines may become in my English a piece of ten lines. I have had to choose between transplanting the physical look of Tamil lines and transposing their patterned internal syntax, and I have invariably chosen the latter course.

In this attempt at rendering the original poems, I have relied on the perceptions and explanations of commentators. I have especially relied on U. Vē. Cāminātaiyar's extraordinarily thorough interpretations and cross-reference in his variorum edition of the text of *Kuṟuntokai* (3rd ed.; Madras: Kapīr Accukkūṭam, 1955).

Transliteration and Pronunciation

The transcription used for Tamil words and names in this book is a strict transliteration. The following Roman letters are used for the corresponding characters in the Tamil alphabet:

Vowels

Short	Long
a	ā
i	ī
u	ū
e	ē
o	ō

Diphthongs

ai au

Consonants

	Lips	Teeth	Ridge Behind Upper Teeth		Hard Palate *Retroflex*	Hard Palate *Palatal*	Soft* Palate
Stops**	p	t			ṭ	c	k
Nasals	m	n	ṉ		ṇ	ñ	ṅ
Liquids			r	l	ḷ		
			ṟ		ṛ		
Semivowels	v					y	

* Approximate place of articulation.
** Manner of articulation.

The charts indicate very roughly the phonetic values of the letters. A few striking features of Tamil pronunciation may be pointed out for the use of readers interested in trying to pronounce the Tamil words the Tamil way.

1. The Tamil long vowels are simple long vowels, unlike their English counterparts, which are diphthongs as in *boat, beat, boot, bate*. Final *-ai* is pronounced *-ey*.

2. Among other things, Tamil has two kinds of consonants unfamiliar to English speakers: the dentals t, n and the retroflexes ṭ, ṇ, ḷ, ṛ. The dentals are pronounced with the tongue stopping the breath at the teeth, positioned somewhat as in *Cyn̲t̲h̲ia*. The retroflexes are made by curling back the tongue towards the roof of the mouth, somewhat as in some American English pronunciations of *par̲t̲y, mor̲n̲ing, gir̲l̲, sir̲*.

3. The Tamil sounds represented by p, t, ṭ, k are not aspirated like English *p̲in, t̲in, k̲in,* but unaspirated as in *sp̲in, st̲ain, sk̲in*.

4. There are long consonants in the middle of Tamil words. English has them only between words: *hot̲ t̲in, seven̲ n̲ights, sick̲ c̲ow,* etc. They are indicated in the text by double letters as in *mul̲l̲ai, eruk̲k̲am*.

5. The Tamil r is flapped or trilled somewhat as in the British pronunciation of *ring, berry*. The ṛ is most like the American variety; r and ṟ are not distinguished in speech by most Tamil speakers today. But doubled ṟṟ is pronounced like tr in English *ṯṟain;* ṉṟ is pronounced ṉḏṟ as in *lauṉḏṟy*.

6. Readers must have noticed the absence of voiced sounds like b, d, j, g and of s, sh, h. The Tamil of the classical period does not represent any of these sounds, though later Tamil orthography found letters for sounds like j, s, h. But p, t, ṭ, c, k serve for these sounds also in certain positions: (A) after nasals, these consonants are voiced into b, d, ḍ, j, g; (B) between vowels p, t, ṭ are voiced into b, d, ḍ and pronounced laxly, but k and c are pronounced h (or g) and s; (C) initially, most Tamilians pronounce c as s. For instance, what is written *caṅkam* is pronounced *sangam, akam* is pronounced *aham* (or *agam*), *kapilar* as *kabilar, kuṟuntokai* as *kurundohey*. There are, of course, dialectal differences.

For oft-used words like *akam, kuṟuntokai,* an approximate pronunciation is suggested in parentheses on their first appearance.

ACKNOWLEDGMENTS

Even a little book has large debts. I am grateful to the many people who made this book possible—colleagues at the South Asia Language and Area Center of the University of Chicago, Edward C. Dimock, Jr., J. A. B. van Buitenen, Milton and Helen Singer; the several Tamil scholars who read my drafts and offered corrections—especially S. A. Pillai, S. P. and E. Annamalai, Kausalya Shenbagam, Kamil Zvelebil; Norman Zide and David Stampe, who suggested changes in the English of the translations; the secretaries who deciphered, typed, and retyped drafts, Mrs. Phyllis Downes, Miss Judith Aronson, Miss Ingrid Kuppershaus; and my wife Molly, whose insights and good taste are in evidence everywhere.

I also thank Mrs. Bonnie R. Crown and Miss Susan Conheim of the Asian Literature Program of the Asia Society, without whose insistent sponsoring the book would never have been put together. They demanded the translation, helped find a publisher, got some of the poems published in periodicals; kept an eye (which winked mischievously sometimes) on the deadlines; and they were kind friends. I need not add: where I have been in error, it is because I have been stubborn.

A. K. R.

Previous Publication of the Poems

The East-West Review, II, 2 (Winter 1965-66)

Kur̲ 41, "When my lover is by my side; *Kur̲* 47, "O long white moonlight"; *Kur̲* 226, "Before I laughed with him"; *Kur̲* 235, "Be good to her, O North Wind"; *Kur̲* 244, "Sir,/not that we did not hear the noise"; *Kur̲* 324, "Maneaters, male crocodiles with crooked legs."

New Mexico Quarterly, XXXV, 4 (Winter 1965-66)

Kur̲ 11, "Bless you, my heart"; *Kur̲* 32, "If one can tell morning"; *Kuṟ* 95, "Where the white waters"; *Kuṟ* 97, "I am here. My virtue"; *Kuṟ* 142, "Does that girl"; *Kuṟ* 157, "Coo Coo"; *Kuṟ* 269, "It would be nice, I think."

Poetry India, I, 1 (January-March 1966)

Kuṟ 46, "Don't they really have"; *Kuṟ* 227, "Here, in the seaside grove"; *Kuṟ* 234, "Only the dim-witted say it's evening"; *Kuṟ* 324, "Man-eaters, male crocodiles with crooked legs."

Prairie Schooner, XXVIII, 2 (Summer 1964)

Kuṟ 32, "If one can tell morning"; *Kuṟ* 138, "The great city fell asleep"; *Kuṟ* 153, "Once: If an owl hooted on the hill"; *Kuṟ* 176, "He did not come just one day"; *Kuṟ* 378, "Let no sun burn."

Prism, IV, 3 (Winter 1965)

Kuṟ 12, "They who know the way he went"; *Kuṟ* 17, "When love is ripe beyond bearing."

The Texas Quarterly, VIII, 1 (Spring 1965)

Kuṟ 6, "The drone of silence"; *Kuṟ* 16, "Will he not really think of us"; *Kuṟ* 42, "Even if passion should pass"; *Kuṟ* 66, "These fat *koṉṟai* trees"; *Kuṟ* 119, "As a little white snake"; *Kuṟ* 234, "Only the dim-witted say its evening."

A. K. Ramanujan, trans., *Fifteen* Poems from a Classical Tamil Anthology* (Calcutta: Writers Workshop, 1965)

Kuṟ 3, "Certainly larger than earth"; *Kuṟ* 7, "This bowman has a warrior-band"; *Kuṟ* 12, "They who know the way he went"; *Kuṟ* 17, "When love is ripe beyond bearing"; *Kuṟ* 18, "O man of the mountain slopes"; *Kuṟ* 32, "If one can tell morning"; *Kuṟ* 40, "What kin was your mother"; *Kuṟ* 67, "Will he remember, friend?"; *Kuṟ* 126, "Friend, when I think"; *Kuṟ* 138, "The great city fell asleep"; *Kuṟ* 153, "Once: if an owl hooted on the hill"; *Kuṟ* 176, "He did not come just one day"; *Kuṟ* 312, "My love is a two-faced thief"; *Kuṟ* 378, "Let no sun burn."

* Only fourteen poems were printed.

The Interior Landscape
THE POEMS

Dramatis Personae

He
She
Her Friend
Her Foster-Mother
Passers-by
Concubine

What She Said

Bigger than earth, certainly,
higher than the sky,
more unfathomable than the waters
is this love for this man

of the mountain slopes
where bees make rich honey
from the flowers of the *kuṟiñci*
that has such black stalks.

Tēvakulattār
Kuṟ 3

What She Said

The still drone of the time
past midnight.
All words put out,
men are sunk into the sweetness
of sleep. Even the far-flung world
has put aside its rages
for sleep.

Only I
am awake.

Patumaṉār
Kuṟ 6

What the Passers-By Said

This bowman has a warrior's band
on his ankle;
the girl with the bracelet on her arm
has a virgin's anklets
on her tender feet.

They look like good people.

In these places
the winds beat
upon the *vākai* trees
and make the white seedpods rattle
like drums for acrobats
dancing on the tightropes.

Poor things, who could they be?
and what makes them walk
with all the others
through these desert ways
so filled with bamboos?

Perumpatumaṉār
Kuṟ 7

What the Concubine Said

You know he comes from
where the fresh-water shark in the pools
catch with their mouths
the mangoes as they fall, ripe
from the trees on the edge of the field.

At our place
he talked big.

Now, back in his own,
when others raise their hands
and feet,
he will raise his too:

like a doll
in a mirror
he will shadow
every last wish
of his son's dear mother.

Ālaṅkuṭi Vaṅkaṉār
Kuṟ 8

What She Said

Bless you, my heart.
The shell bangles slip
from my wasting hands.
My eyes, sleepless for days,
are muddied.
        Get up, let's go, let's get out
        of this loneliness here.

Let's go
where the tribes wear
the narcotic wreaths of *cannabis*
beyond the land of *Kaṭṭi,*
the chieftain with many spears,
        let's go, I say,
        to where my man is,

        enduring even
        alien languages.

Māmūlaṉār
Kuṟ 11

What She Said

People who know the way he went
say: where he goes now,
the *Eyiṉar* tribes with the bent bows
whet the points of their arrows;
cross water-passes in the mountain
which are like tunnels in an anthill;
climb rocks
hot as a blacksmith's anvil;
and the road has many branches.

But this loud-mouthed town
knows nothing of my fears
about the hardship of his ways,
and taunts me
for being lovesick.

Ōtalāntaiyār
Kuṟ 12

What the Foster-Mother Said

He had a beautiful war bracelet
and his white spear
had a red tongue
for a blade,
and she had many bangles
on her hand.

Her love has come true
like the infallible word
of the *Kōcars* from the four villages
gathered under the ancient banyan;

as the wedding drums thunder,
and the conch-shell trumpets blare,

her love is made good and true.

Auvaiyār
Kur̲ 15

What Her Friend Said

Will he not really think of us
when he passes the clumps of milk-hedge
with their fragrant trunks
and hears the redlegged lizard call
to his mate
in cluckings that sound like
the highway robber's fingernail
testing the point of his iron arrow,
will he not really think of us, friend?

Pālaipāṭiya Peruṅkaṭuṅkō
Kuṟ 16

What He Said

When love is ripe beyond bearing
and goes to seed,
men will ride even palmyra stems
like horses; will wear on their heads
the reeking cones of the *erukkam* bud
like flowers; will draw to themselves
the gossip of the streets;

and will do worse.

Pēreyiṉ Muṟuvalār
Kuṟ 17

What Her Friend Said to Him

O man of the mountain slopes
where the jackfruit tree has fruit almost on its roots
with the small live bamboo for its fences,
be of good thoughts and think of marriage.
No one knows of her state.

She's like those other trees on the slopes,
their giant jacks hanging
from slender boughs:
her breath is short,
and her love great beyond bearing.

Kapilar
Kuṟ 18

What She Said

It looks as if the summer's glowing
new blossom on the dark neem tree
will not stay for his coming.

These cruel women's tongues
are working on me,
now that he is gone,
grinding me to paste
like the one fig
of the white tree rising by the waterside,
trampled on by seven ravenous crabs.

Paraṇar
Kuṟ 24

What She Said

Only the thief was there, no one else.
And if he should lie, what can I do?

There was only
a thin-legged heron standing
on legs yellow as millet stems
and looking
for lampreys
in the running water
when he took me.

Kapilar
Kuṟ 25

What She Said

Shall I charge like a bull
against this sleepy town,
or try beating it with sticks,
or cry wolf
till it is filled with cries
of Ah's and Oh's?

It knows nothing, and sleeps
through all my agony, my sleeplessness,
and the swirls of this swaying south wind.

O what shall I do
to this dump of a town!

Auvaiyār
Kuṟ 28

What She Said

My lover capable of terrible lies
at night lay close to me
in a dream
that lied like truth.

I woke up, still deceived,
and caressed the bed
thinking it my lover.

It's terrible. I grow lean
in loneliness,
like a water lily
gnawed by a beetle.

Kaccipēṭṭu Naṉṉākaiyār
Kuṟ 30

What She Said

Nowhere, not among the warriors at their festival,
nor with the girls dancing close in pairs,
nowhere did I see my lover.

I am a dancer;
my pride, my lover,
                    —for love of him
                    these conch-shell bangles slip
                    from my wasting hands—
he's a dancer too.

Ātimantiyār
Kuṟ 31

What He Said

If one can tell morning
from noon from listless evening,
the night of sleeping towns from dawn,
then one's love
is a lie.
                    If I should lose her
I could proclaim my misery in the streets
riding mock horses on palmyra stems in my wildness:
but that seems such a shame.

                                        But then, even living,
away from her, seems such a shame.

Aḷḷūr Naṉmullaiyār
Kuṟ 32

What She Said

about the messenger from her lover

This singer is still a young student.
And how good he must sound
in the public places
of his own town!

Eating what others give,
his face is not filled out.

And his talent
is looking for fresh feasts.

Paṭumarattu Mōcikīraṉār
Kuṟ 33

What She Said

On his hills,
    the *māṇai* creeper that usually sprawls
    on large round stones
    sometimes takes to a sleeping elephant.

At parting,
    his arms twined with mine
    he gave me inviolable guarantees
    that he would live in my heart
    without parting.

Friend, why do you think
    that is any reason for grieving?

Paraṇar
Kuṟ 36

What He Said

What could my mother be
to yours? What kin is my father
to yours anyway? And how
did you and I meet ever?
                    But in love our hearts are as red
earth and pouring rain:
                    mingled
beyond parting.

Cempulappeyan̲īrār
Kur̲ 40

What She Said

When my lover is by my side
I am happy
as a city
in the rapture of a carnival,

and when he is gone
I grieve like a deserted house
in a little hamlet
of the wastelands

where the squirrel plays
in the front yard.

Aṇilāṭu Mu<u>nr</u>ilār
Ku<u>r</u> 41

What Her Friend Said to Him

Even if passion should pass,
O man of the hills
where
after the long tempestuous rains
of night
the morning's waterfalls
make music in the caverns,
would our love also pass
with the passion?

Kapilar
Kuṟ 42

What She Said

Don't they really have
in the land where he has gone
such things
as house sparrows

dense-feathered, the color of fading water lilies,
pecking at grain drying on yards,
playing with the scatter of the fine dust
of the streets' manure
and living with their nestlings
in the angles of the penthouse

and miserable evenings,

and loneliness?

Māmalāṭan̲
Kur̲ 46

What Her Girl-Friend Said

O long white moonlight,
you do him no good at all
as he comes stealing
through the night in the forest

where the black-stemmed *vēṅkai*
drops its flowers
on the round stones
and makes them look
like tiger cubs
in the half-light!

Neṭuveṇṇilaviṉār
Kuṟ 47

What He Said in the Desert

The marauding wolf
has gouged here and drunk
of this little stagnant water,
now mantled over
by the wild jasmine.

How I wish my girl,
my heart's mistress, her hands all bangles,
were here with me
to share even this:
                    but it would be pitiful
                    if she were.

Ciṟaikkuṭiyāntaiyār
Kuṟ 56

What Her Friend Said

Like youngsters
who get all their joy
by just drawing with their hands
a toy cart and a carpenter's wooden horse,
without ever mounting anything life-size,

our girl is happy still
though she has had no pleasure from her man.
Her bangles are not yet slipping
from her hands,
for she lives in the thought
of her love
who has great pools
and chariots.

Tumpicērkīraṉ
Kuṟ 61

What Her Girl-Friend Said to Her

These fat *konrai* trees
are gullible:

> the season of rains
> that he spoke of
> when he went through the stones
> of the desert
> is not yet here
>
> though these trees
> mistaking the untimely rains
> have put out
> their long arrangements of flowers
> on the twigs
>
> as if for a proper monsoon.

Kōvatattaṉ
Kuṟ 66

What She Said

Will he remember, friend?
Where the curve of the parrot's beak
holds a bright-lit neem
like the sharp glory
of a goldsmith's nail
threading a coin of gold
for a new jewel,

he went across the black soil
and the cactus desert.

Will he remember?

Aḷḷūr Naṉmullai
Kuṟ 67

What She Said

The bare root of the bean is pink
like the leg of a jungle hen,
and herds of deer attack its overripe pods.

For the harshness of this early frost
there is no cure

but the breast of my man.

Aḷḷūr Naṉmullai
Kuṟ 68

What Her Friend Said to Her

Our man of the hills

    where the bent green bamboo springs back to the sky
    with the spring of an unleashed horse

grows thin longing for our love,
like a tethered bull in summertime,

not knowing that here we are, wasting away
for his sake.

Viṭṭakutiraiyār
Kuṟ 74

What She Said to the Messenger

Tell me:

did you really see him
or did you just hear it from someone
who did see him?
I want to make sure.

May you get *Pātali* City
filled with gold
where white-tuskers
play in the *Cōṇai* River!

But tell me first:
from whose mouth
did you hear
of my lover's coming?

Patumarattu Mōcikīraṉār
Kuṟ 75

What He Said

Where the white waters from the peak
crash through the mountain caves,
it flowers on the slopes;
                    and there, the little hill-town chieftain
                    has a younger daughter, a girl
                    with great arms, and she is tender as water;

                    fancy her quelling my fire!

Kapilar
Kuṟ 95

What She Said

I am here. My virtue
lies in grief
in the groves near the sea.
                              My lover
is back in his hometown. And our secret
is with the gossips
in public places.

Veṇpūti
Kuṟ 97

What She Said

It would help, dear friend,
if we could get someone
to go to him
with some of those rain flowers

    of the sponge gourd
    that grows so lush
    with leaves among the tall wet grasses
    on our farm

and tell him: Look,
the girl's fair brow
has yellowed like these
with love.

Kōkkuḷamuṟṟaṉ
Kuṟ 98

What He Said

O did I not think of you?
and thinking of you,
did I not think and think again of you?
and even as I thought of you
was I not baffled
by the world's demands
that held me to my work?

O love, did I not think of you,
and think of you till I wished
I were here to sate my passion
till this flood of desire
that once wet the branch of the tall tree
would thin
till I can bend and scoop a drink of water
with my hands?

Auvaiyār
Kuṟ 99

What She Said

Look, friend,
fear of scandal will only thin out passion.
And if I should just give up my love
to end this dirty talk,
I will be left
only with my shame.

My virgin self of which he partook
is now like a branch half broken
by an elephant,
bent, not yet fallen to the ground,
still attached to the mother tree
by the fiber of its bark.

Ālattūrkiḷār
Kuṟ 112

What He Said

As a little white snake
with lovely stripes on its young body
troubles the jungle elephant
        this slip of a girl
        her teeth like sprouts of new rice
        her wrists stacked with bangles
        troubles me.

Catti Nātaṉār
Kuṟ 119

What Her Girl-Friend Said

The sands are like heaped-up moonlight.
Right next to it stands all by itself,
as if all night were crammed into it,
the cool dense shade of a flowering grove
of the black *pu<u>nn</u>ai*.

Our man has not come back.

Only our brothers' fishing boats
will return from their hunt
of many kinds of fish.

Aiyūr Muṭava<u>n</u>
Ku<u>r</u> 123

What Her Girl-Friend Said to Him

You say that the wasteland
you have to pass through
is absence itself:
wide spaces where sometimes
salt merchants have gathered for a while
and gone, *ōmai* trees that stand
like ghost towns once busy with living.

But tell me really,
do you think that home will be sweet
for the ones you leave behind?

Pālaipāṭiya Peruṅkaṭuṅkō
Kuṟ 124

What She Said

Friend,

with no regard for youth
in search of riches he went
no one knows where,
and he will not come back.

Her teeth of jasmine
strung on the rain-shadowed creeper,
this season of cool rains
will laugh.

Okkūr Mācātti
Kuṟ 126

What Her Friend Said to Her

He just cannot have dug and entered the earth,
   nor climbed the skies,
nor waded barefoot through all those seas
   he must have met;

If only one looks for him in land after land,
            from town to town,
family by family, our lover
cannot slip through the cordon, can he?

Veḷḷi Vītiyār
Kuṟ 130

What He Said

Her arms have the beauty
of a gently moving bamboo.
Her eyes are full of peace.
She is faraway,
her place not easy to reach.

My heart is frantic
with haste,
        a plowman with a single ox
        on land all wet
        and ready for seed.

Ōrēruṛavaṉār
Kuṟ 131

What He Said

Love, love,
they say. Yet love
is no new grief
nor sudden disease; nor something
that rages and cools.
        Like madness in an elephant,
        coming up when he eats
        certain leaves,

        love waits
        for you to find
        someone to look at.

Miḷaipperuṅkantaṉ
Kuṟ 136

What Her Friend Said

The great city fell asleep
but we did not sleep.
Clearly we heard, all night,
from the hillock next to our house
the tender branches of the flower-clustered tree
with leaves like peacock feet
let fall
their blue-sapphire flowers.

Kollaṉ Aḻici
Kuṟ 138

What He Said

Does that girl,
                    eyes like flowers, gathering flowers
from pools for her garlands, driving away the parrots
from the millet fields,
                         does that girl know at all
or doesn't she,
                    that my heart is still there with her
                    bellowing sighs
                    like a drowsy midnight elephant?

Kapilar
Kuṟ 142

What She Said

These fault-finders,
they know nothing:

love is like the young of the tortoise
nourished by the sight
of its mother.
                    What else is left
but to dry up and rot within
like an abandoned egg

if he should leave me
to my own devices?

Kiḷimaṅkalaṅkiṛār
Kuṟ 152

What She Said

Once: if an owl hooted on the hill,
if a male ape leaped and loped
out there on the jackfruit bough in our yard
my poor heart would melt for fear. But now
                in the difficult dark of night
                nothing can stay its wandering
                on the long sloping mountain-ways
                of his coming.

Kapilar
Kuṟ 153

What She Said

Co Coo
crowed the cock
and my poor heart missed a beat
that the sword of morning came down
to cut me off from my lover
twined in my arms

Aḷḷūr Naṉmullai
Kuṟ 157

What Her Friend Said

He did not come just one day: he did not come
  just two days.
But many days he came and softened my good heart
with many modest words said many times. And
      like a honeycomb ripening on the hills
      suddenly falling
      he went.

Where is our man, good as a father, on whom we leaned?
      As from rainstorms pouring
      on a distant green land
my heart runs muddy.

Varumulaiyāritti
Kuṟ 176

What She Said

The rains, already old,
have brought new leaf upon the fields.
The grass spears are trimmed and blunted
by the deer.
The jasmine creeper is showing its buds
through their delicate calyx
like the laugh of a wildcat.

In jasmine country, it is evening
for the hovering bees,
but look, he hasn't come back.

He left me and went in search
of wealth.

Okkūr Mācātti
Kuṟ 220

What She Said

My lover has not come back:
the jasmine has blossomed.

A goat-herd comes into town
with goats and milk
to take some rice to the others

waiting outside,
palmyra rain-guards in their hands,
herds of young ones in their care:

in his hair
nothing but tiny buds
of jasmine.

Uṟaiyūr Mutukoṟṟaṉ
Kuṟ 221

What He Said

about her and her friend

If her girl-friend should take the head of the raft
my girl will also take the head.
If the rear
my girl will take the rear.
And if her friend should let go
and go with the stream,
it looks as if
she will go too.

Her eyes are cool, full-bodied
buds of the dewy rain flower
streaked with red,
and she is the new leaf
in the rain.

Ciṟaikkuṭiyāntaiyār
Kuṟ 222

What She Said to Her Girl-Friend

Once you said
let's go, let's go
to the gay carnival in the big city;

that day
the good elders spoke of many good omens
for our going.

But he waylaid me,
gave me a slingshot and rattles
for scaring parrots,
and a skirt of young leaves
which he said looked good
on me,

and with his lies
he took the rare innocence
that mother had saved for me.

And now I am like this.

Maṯuraikkaṭaiyattār Makan Veṇṇākaṉ
Kuṟ 223

What She Says

about her friend's sympathy

This is worse than the sleepless agony
of thinking about him, far away,
wandering long among the trees
through difficult branching pathways.

This is much worse: I cannot bear to think
of my friend's grief for me,

it's like the deaf-mute's
when he sees at night the suffering
of a dun cow fallen into a well.

Kūvan Maintan̲
Kur̲ 224

What She Said

Before I laughed with him
        nightly,

        the slow waves beating
        on his wide shores
        and the palmyra
        bringing forth heron-like flowers
        near the waters,

my eyes were like the lotus
my arms had the grace of the bamboo
my forehead was mistaken for the moon.

        But now

Maturai Eṟuttāḷaṉ Cēntampūtaṉ
Kuṟ 226

What Her Girl-Friend Said

In the seaside grove
where he drove back in his chariot
the *neytal* flowers are on the ground,
some of their thick petals plowed in
and their stalks broken

by the knife-edge of his wheels' golden rims
furrowing the earth.

Ōta Ñāni
Kuṟ 227

What She Said

Only the dim-witted say it's evening
        when the sun goes down
        and the sky reddens,
        when misery deepens,
        and the *mullai* begins to bloom
        in the dusk.

But even when the tufted cock
        calls in the long city
        and the long night
        breaks into dawn,
        it is evening:
                        even noon
        is evening,

        to the companionless.

Miḷaipperuṅ Kantaṉ
Kuṟ 234

What He Said

Be good to her, O North Wind,
and may you prosper!

There, among thin silver rills
that look like hanging snake skins,

high on the hill

where herds of elk
plunder the gooseberry
in the courtyards,
there
lies my good woman's village
of grass-thatched cottages.

Māyeṇṭan
Kuṟ 235

What She Said

My friend,
I will not think again of him,

of his long seashore
noisy with birds

the *aṭumpu* creeper with leaves cloven
as the hooves of a deer,
the bright-bangled women
prying open for their games
its flowers that look like the shiny beads and bells
on a horse's neck,

and I will let my eyes sleep.

Nampi Kuṭṭuvan
Kuṟ 243

What Her Girl-Friend Said to Him

Sir,
   not that we did not hear the noise
   you made trying to open the bolted doors,
   a robust bull elephant
   stirring in the night
   of everyone's sleep;

we did. But as we fluttered inside
like a peacock in the net,
crest broken, tail feathers flying,

our good mother held us close
in her innocence
thinking to quell our fears.

Kaṇṇaṉ
Kuṟ 244

What Her Girl-Friend Said

when she sees that her friend's love-sickness is being misunderstood and rites of exorcism are performed to cure her

Cutting the throat of a sacrificial goat,
    offering special platters of grain,
    and sounding many instruments on the dry islets
    in a running river,*

none of this will help: they'll put on a show,
but will bring no remedy
for our girl's disease.

And this calling on all the great gods
    except the right one, her lover,
    as if some demon
    possessed her—

    it's really painful,

    when she is only being faithful
    to her secret lover
    from the tall hills where
    the clouds play games.

Peruñcāttaṉ
Kuṟ 263

* The Tamil phrase may also mean "at the crossroads in the busy highways."

What She Said

It would be nice, I think,
if someone didn't mind
the hurry and the long walk,
and went to give him the good word:

> the wound that father got
> pulling in that big shark
> is healed and he's gone back
> to the blue-dark of the sea;
>
> and mother's gone to the salt pans
> to sell her salt for white rice;

if only someone would reach my man
on his cold wide shore and tell him:
    this is the time to come!

Kallāṭaṉār
Kuṟ 269

What She Said

My man
of the roaring waters
that scatter whole waterfalls,
I knew him and was with him
only for a day

but it has been part of my arms
for many days now
and turned into a disease
that ravages all beauty.

Aṛici Naccāttaṉār
Kuṟ 271

What He Said to Himself in the Desert

Here, the trunk of the *ukāy* tree is soft
as the back of a dove, and its beads of fruit
are shaken down
as the bandit,
his arrow readied in the bow,
climbs high places
on the look-out for passers-by

chewing on a surrogate bark
in the desert
for want of water.

Even these wilds may grow sweet
if only I can keep my mind's eye steady
as I go
on my love's mound-of-venus
jeweled by gold and beads,

or simply
on her lovely breasts.

Uruttiraṉ
Kuṟ 274

What Her Girl-Friend Said to Her

Come, let's go climb on that jasmine-mantled rock
        and look

if it is only the evening cowbells
of the grass-fed contented herds
returning with the bulls

or the bells of his chariot
driving back through the wet sand of the
                forest ways,
his heart full of the triumph of a job
                well done,
with young archers driving by his side.

Okkūr Mācātti
Kuṟ 275

What He Said

in exasperation when her girl-friend refused him access to his love

I sewed and made
for my bamboo-shouldered girl
a patchwork doll like herself

with sedge grass and things
from the edges of the pools
where we roamed.

Yet they'll acknowledge nothing,
these bodyguards of hers,
not even the beauty streaks
I've painted on her arrogant rising breasts!

Wait till I ask for her
in the sceptred court of our moral king
and see what happens then

to this rotten townful of girl-friends,
all of them utter fools!
It's just pitiful.

Kōṛikkoṟṟaṉ
Kuṟ 276

What She Said to Her Girl-Friend

You, wearing red gold!

Our man went there:
where the forest has joined the hills
wearing in the spiral glory of her hair

a white sprig of the desert neem's flowers
arranged in the calyx of the white crown leaves

of the palmyra, jagged, yellow-trunked,
rising on the white sands.

Kuṭavāyir̠ Kīrattan̠
Kur̠ 281

What She Said to Her Friend

Where the pepper vine grows
and troops of monkeys
live off the young leaves,

among his cliffs he stays,
far away; he is a sweet man, yet.

And tell me, is even the so-called sweet heaven
sweeter, really, than the affliction
that dear ones bring?

Kapilar
Kuṟ 288

What She Said

People say, “You will have to bear it.”
    Don’t they know what passion is like,
    or is it that they are so strong?

As for me, if I do not see my lover
    grief drowns my heart,

    and like a streak of foam in high waters
    dashed on the rocks

    little by little I ebb
    and become nothing.

Kalporu Ciṟunuraiyār
Kuṟ 290

What Her Girl-Friend Said

When a lovely girl bathing in a river
ate a green mango from his tree
floated by the water,
for that crime
King *Naṉṉaṉ* would take nothing,
not even an offer of
nine times nine bull elephants
and the girl's weight in gold
moulded as a doll,

but just killed her.
Like him,
may this mother, too, go to everlasting hell!

For, the other day, when our girl's lover
just came in
as a guest with a smiling face,
this woman wouldn't sleep for days

as if she were a city on an enemy line.

Paraṇar
Kuṟ 292

What She Said

O friend, drunkards make pilgrimages
into Āti Arumāṉ's ancient city
and bring back kernels
from the tall black palm, its spathes full
    of fibrous fruit;

she is like that city, his harlot.
Her full skirts of white water-flower wreaths
move alternately
on her thighs marked with love's pallor,
and she has gold on her.
                            And she comes to see
my husband here.
                    Pity me, I need it.

Kaḻḻilāttiraiyaṉ
Kuṟ 293

What Her Girl-Friend Said to Her

about her careless lover

If,
when you play water games
or stay in seaside groves
or dance in flowers
those linked dances with your girl-friends

he comes and leaves
as he does,
without ceremony, like a neighbor
after making love,
naturally there would be talk.

Now it's blown over.
Still he is never far away
from that side-skirt of green leaves,
those artful jewels that shake
on your venus' mound

now spread like a cobra hood
and touched by love's pallor.

No wonder your mother stands guard over you:
he brought it on himself.

Añcilāntai
Kuṟ 294

What Her Girl-Friend Said to the Unfaithful Husband

Your mistresses wear the green leaf
for skirt, earring and garland; they even
sport leaves in their hair.

You play with whole gangs of them
and come home with the relics
of your water carnivals
all over you.

This town has begun to say,
once this fellow lived off
a single wretched cow;
now, since the windfall
his little woman brought him

he has carnivals.

Tūṅkalōri
Kuṟ 295

What She Said to Her Girl-Friend

On beaches washed by seas
older than the earth,
in the groves filled with bird-cries,
on the banks shaded by a *puṉṉai*
clustered with flowers,
                when we made love
my eyes saw him
and my ears heard him;

my arms grow beautiful
in the coupling
and grow lean
as they come away.
                What shall I make of this?

Veṇmaṇippūṭi
Kuṟ 299

What He Said

My love is a two-faced thief.
In the dead of night
she comes like the fragrance
of the Red-Speared Chieftain's forest hills,
to be one with me.

And then, she sheds the petals
of night's several flowers,
and does her hair again
with new perfumes and oils,
to be one with her family at dawn

with a stranger's different face.

Kapilar
Kuṟ 312

What Her Girl-Friend Said to Him

when he wanted to come by night

Man-eaters, male crocodiles with crooked legs,
cut off the traffic on these waterways.
                                        But you,
in your love, will come to her swimming
through the shoals of fish in the black salt marshes.
                                        And she,
she will suffer in her simpleness.
                                        And I,
what can I do but shudder in my heart
like a woman watching her poisoned twins?

Kavaimakaṉ
Kuṟ 324

What Her Foster-Mother Said

Let no sun burn
may trees shade the little ways on the hill
may the paths be covered with sand
may cool rain
cool the desert roads
    for that simple girl
    her face the color of the new mango leaf
    who left us
    for a man
    with the long bright spear!

Kaymaṉār
Kuṟ 378

The Interior Landscape
AFTERWORD

Afterword

Classical Tamil

Tamil, one of the two classical languages of India, is the only language of contemporary India which is recognizably continuous with a classical past. Today this Dravidian* language is spoken by 31 million Indians, mainly in Madras state in the southeast region of peninsular India. It is also spoken outside India as a mother tongue, chiefly in Ceylon and Malaya, and by small groups in Burma, parts of Africa, the Fiji Islands, and the West Indies.

Early classical Tamil literature is represented by eight anthologies of lyrics, ten long poems, and a grammar called the *Tolkāppiyam* (pronounced *Tolhāppiyam*), meaning the "Old Composition." The poems in the present book are selections from the anthology of love lyrics called the *Kuṟuntokai* (pronounced *Kurundohey*), one of the earliest anthologies to have survived.

At least six of the eight anthologies appear to have been compiled, if not composed, during the first three centuries

* Tamil is the oldest of the four major Dravidian languages of contemporary South India. The others are Kannada, Malayalam, and Telugu, which according to the census of 1961 are spoken by 18, 17, and 38 millions in Mysore, Kerala, and Andhra Pradesh states respectively. At least 17 other nonliterary Dravidian languages are scattered all over central, eastern, and western India, the farthest-flung being Brahui, a Dravidian speech-island in today's Pakistan, surrounded by Indo-Aryan and Indo-Iranian languages of the Northwest.

of the Christian era. The evidence for such dating comes from various sources: archeological finds of Roman coins; tallies between Greek traveler-historians and the Tamil texts, especially the "war" poems; references in the colophons to the poems; textual reconstructions from cross-references to poets and patron-kings; and lastly from the linguistic peculiarities of the poems.*

Early classical Tamil is not intelligible to a modern Tamilian without special study. From the earliest times there appear to have been two varieties of Tamil in use, a formal variety, probably written later, and an informal variety with many spoken dialects.

Today formal Tamil is more conservative than the informal and therefore closer to earlier Tamil. The development of verb- and noun-endings, losses and gains in vocabulary, and the influence of other languages like Sanskrit and English have widened the distance between ancient and modern Tamil.

Caṅkam (pronounced Sangam)

The literature of Classical Tamil later came to be known as *Caṅkam* literature. *Caṅkam* means "an academy or fraternity." The word is probably borrowed from the vocabulary of Buddhism or Jainism, the two religions competing with Hinduism around the sixth and seventh centuries in South India. A seventh-century commentator applied the term to poets and spoke of three academies or *Caṅkams* of poets under the patronage of *Pāṇḍya* kings. He also asserted that the three *Caṅkams* lasted 4,440, 3,700, and 1,850 years** respectively, and that they included immortal gods, sages, and kings as member poets. A whole

* There are unresolved controversies among historians on these questions. A summary of the complicated arguments may be followed in a standard work of history. See K. A. Nilakanta Sastri, *A History of South India,* Oxford Univ. Press, 1958.

** It has been pointed out that these numbers are suspicously regular multiples of 37: the Jains had a passion for numbers.

mythology has grown up around these poems, and in particular the myth of antediluvian kingdoms extending back many millennia and of a large body of works lost in a Great Flood. It is possible that there were schools of poets in certain courts and the Flood Legends about these schools may be a way of saying that the few surviving texts are from a long and lost tradition of poetic composition.

The grammar *Tolkāppiyam* was assigned to the second *Caṅkam,* the eight anthologies and the ten long poems to the third; no extant work has been assigned to the first *Caṅkam.*

The Anthologies

Caṅkam verse varies in length from 4 to over 800 lines. There are 2,389 *Caṅkam* poems, of which about 100 are anonymous. Four hundred sixty-one poets are known by proper names or by epithets. In the *Kuṟuntokai,* there are 400 love poems. These are assigned to 205 poets, but of these 205, 13 are named after a striking phrase or metaphor in the poems assigned to them. Poem 40 is by Cempulappeyaṉīrār, which would mean "The Poet of the Red Earth and Pouring Rain." Poem 47 is by Neṭuveṇṇilaviṉār, "The Poet of the Long White Moonlight." The classical tradition of Tamil poetry is an impersonal tradition. The use of epithetical names seems to suggest that for these poets no signature was more authentic than their own metaphors.

In the rhetoric and in the anthologies the poems were classified by their themes as *akam* and *puṟam. Akam* meant "inner part," *puṟam* "outer part." *Akam* poems were love poems; *puṟam* poems were "public" poems on war, kings, death, etc. The two types of poems had differing proprieties, as we shall see below, though the same poets often wrote both kinds of poems. The eight anthologies and their contents, excluding opening invocations that were added later, were as follows:

Akam Anthologies

1. *Kuṟuntokai,* 400 love poems, 4-9 lines each
2. *Naṟṟiṇai,* 400 love poems, 9-12 lines each
3. *Akanāṉūṟu,* 400 love poems, 13-37 lines each
4. *Aiṅkuṟuṉūṟu,* 500 love poems, each hundred dealing with one of the five conventional phases of love and apparently written by a different poet
5. *Kalittokai,* love poems in a metre called *kali*

Puṟam Anthologies

6. *Puṟanāṉūṟu,* 400 *puṟam* poems
7. *Patiṟṟuppattu,* the "Ten Tens," 100 poems on kings (with the first ten and the tenth ten missing)
8. *Paripāṭal,* the only collection of *Caṅkam* poems on religious themes.

Kalittokai and *Paripāṭal* appear to be the latest of the eight anthologies; *Kuṟuntokai* and *Puṟanāṉūṟu* contain probably the earliest compositions.

The Tolkāppiyam

The grammar called the *Tolkāppiyam* is the most important expository text for the understanding of early Tamil poetry. It is not only a grammar of the Tamil of that time but also a work of rhetoric. It has three sections corresponding to phonology, morphology, and semantics: (a) Sounds, (b) Words, (c) Meaning. In the third section, the author sets down the canons of the *Caṅkam* poetic tradition.

According to legend and according to some modern scholars, the grammar antedates the *Caṅkam* poems. But the conventions of the *Caṅkam* poems do not seem to be the outcome of a work of rhetoric. The rhetorician summarized what was a live and continuing tradition. Because of the strength of this tradition some 500 poets appear to share to an unusual degree the poetic prescriptions of the *Tol-*

kāppiyam. The rhetoric behind the poetry is outlined below.

Like many other Indian expository texts, this work is presented as a series of *cūttirams* (Sanskrit *sūtra*), or brief verse-sayings. Paraphrases of relevant excerpts from the chapter on love poetry will be cited and identified by the number of the *cūttiram*.

Akam and Puṟam

Caṅkam poetry, as was noted, is classified by theme into two kinds: poems of *akam* (the "inner part" or the Interior) and poems of *puṟam* (the "outer part" or the Exterior). *Akam* poems are love poems; *puṟam* poems are all other kinds of poems, usually about good and evil, action, community, kingdom; it is the "public" poetry of the ancient Tamils, celebrating the ferocity and glory of kings, lamenting the death of heroes, the poverty of poets. Elegies, panegyrics, invectives, poems on wars and tragic events are *puṟam* poems.

Unlike *akam* poems, *puṟam* poems may mention explicitly the names of kings and poets and places. The poem is placed in a real society and given a context of real history. *Akam* poems tends to focus attention on a spare single image; in *puṟam* poems, the images rush and tumble over one another. Here are a few examples of the *puṟam* genre:

What a Hero's Mother Said

You stand against the pillar
of my hut and ask me:
Where is your son?

I don't really know.
My womb is only a lair
for that tiger.
You can see him now
only in battlefields.

Puṟanāṉuṟu
(The Four Hundred *Puṟam* Poems) 87

The King in Combat

With the festival hour close at hand
his woman in labor
a sun setting behind pouring rains

the needle in the cobbler's hand
is in a frenzy of haste
stitching thongs for the cot of a king:

such was the swiftness
of the Great *Cōḷa's* tackles,
an *atti* garland round his neck,
as he wrestled with the enemy
come all the way
to take the land.

Pu͟ranā͟nū͟ru 82

In Praise of a King

Fish leaping
in fields of sheep.
Rash unplowed sowing
in the haunts of the wild boar.
Big-eyed buffalo herds
stopped by lilies in sugarcane beds.

Ancient cows bend
over water flowers
where once busy dancers
did the Devil's Mask.

The tall coconut, the sounding *marutam**
now feed
the mouth of a stream
and a flowering pool.

Gone are the villages
sung in song. Faces
of terror instead of beauty,

they look like a corpse
killed and stood up
by Death.

* A tree.

For your rage
water and village are one;
waves of sugarcane blossom
are one stalk of grass.
The ashen babul** of the twisted fruit
twined with the giant black babul,
the she-devil with the branching crest
roams
astraddle on the donkey;
and the small persistent thorn
is spread in the moving dust of battlefields.

The dead hearts of public places are filled
with dirt and turds and silence,
and the ruins chill
all courage and desire.

But here,
the sages have sought your woods.
In open spaces the fighters play
with their bright-jewelled women.
The traveller is safe on the highway.
The sellers of grain shelter their dear kin
and shelter even the distant kin.
The Silver Star will not go near
the place of Mars. And it rains
on the thirsty fields. Hunger has fled
and taken Disease with her. O Great One,

in your land it blossoms
everywhere.

Patirruppattu (The Ten Tens), Poem 13

Akam or Love Poetry

Akam poetry is directly about experience, not action; it is a poetry of the "inner world."

In *Akattiṇai Iyal* or the chapter on *akam* poetry, the *Tolkāppiyam* distinguishes *akam* and *puṟam* conventions

** A bush.

as follows: "In the five phases of *akam,** no names of persons should be mentioned. Particular names are appropriate only in *puṟam* poetry." The dramatis personae for *akam* are idealized types, such as chieftains representing clans and classes, rather than historical persons. Similarly, landscapes are more important than particular places.

The love of man and woman is taken as the ideal expression of the "inner world," and *akam* poetry is synonymous with love poetry in the Tamil tradition. Love in all its variety—love in separation and in union, before and after marriage, in chastity and in betrayal—is the theme of *akam*. "There are seven types of love, of which the first is *kaikkiḻai,* unrequited love, and the last is *peruntiṇai,* mismatched love [1]." *Peruntiṇai* or the Major Type (as the *Tolkāppiyam* somewhat cynically calls it) of man-woman relationship is the forced, loveless relationship: a man and a woman, mismatched in age, coming together for duty, convenience, or lust. At the other extreme is *kaikkiḷai* (literally the Base Relationship), the one-sided affair, unrequited love, or desire inflicted on an immature girl who does not understand it. Neither of these extremes is the proper subject of *akam* poetry. They are common, abnormal, undignified, fit only for servants. "Servants and workmen are outside the five *akam* types [of true love], for they do not have the necessary strength of character [25-26]." Most of the *akam* anthologies contain no poems of unrequited or mismatched love; only *Kalittokai* has a number of examples of both types.

Of the seven types, only "the middle five" are the subject of true love poetry. The hero and heroine should be "well-matched in ten points," such as beauty, wealth, age, virtue, rank, etc. Only such a pair is capable of the full range of love: union and separation, anxiety and patience, betrayal and forgiveness. The couple must be cultured; for the uncultured will be rash, ignorant, self-centered, and therefore unfit for *akam* poetry.

* For the five phases, see p. 105.

The Five Landscapes

In the chapter on *akam* poetry *Tolkāppiyam* concerns itself mainly with the "middle five" phases or types of love and outlines their symbolic conventions. "When we examine the materials of a poem, only three things appear to be important: mutal (the First Things), *karu* (the Native Elements), *uri* (the Human Feelings appropriately set in *mutal* and *karu*) [3]." "What are called *mutal* or First Things are time and place; so say the people who know [4.]" There are four kinds of "place"; each is presided over by a deity and named for a flower or tree characteristic of the region:

Mullai, a variety of jasmine, stands for the forests overseen by *Māyōn,* the dark-bodied god of herdsmen;

Kuṟiñci (pronounced *kurinji*), a mountain flower, for the mountains overseen by *Murukaṉ,* the red-speared god of war, youth, and beauty;

Marutam (pronounced *marudam,* the ḏ being dental as in the English *t̲h̲en*), a tree with red flowers growing near the water, for the pastoral region, overseen by *Vēntaṉ,* the rain-god;

Neytal (pronounced *neydal,* the ḏ being dental), a water flower, for the sandy seashore overseen by the wind-god [5].

A fifth region, *pālai* or desert waste, is also mentioned. *Pālai* is given no specific location, for it is said that any mountain or forest may be parched to a wasteland in the heat of summer. It is named for *pālai,* supposedly an evergreen tree unaffected by drought.*

Time is divided into day, month, and year. The year is divided into six "large time-units," the six seasons: the rains, the cold season, early frost and late frost, early summer and late summer. The day is divided into five "small

* Some of the eight anthologies are explicitly arranged according to these five types of landscape, though *Kuṟuntokai* is not. For instance *Aiṅkuṟunūṟu* has a hundred poems for each of the types.

time-units": sunrise, midday, sunset, nightfall, the dead of night. Some would add a sixth, dawn.

Particular large and small time-units are associated by convention with particular regions. "*Mullai* country is associated with the rainy season and evening; *kuṟiñci,* with the early frost and midnight; *marutam,* with the later part of night and the dawn; *neytal,* with the twilight of evening; *pālai,* with summer, late frost, and midday [6-12]."

Each of the five regions or landscapes is associated further with an appropriate *uri,* or phase of love.

> Lovers' union is associated with *kuṟiñci,* the mountains;
> separation with *pālai,* the desert;
> patient waiting with *mullai,* the forests;
> anxious waiting with *neytal,* the seashore;
> the lover's infidelity and the beloved's resentment
>   with *marutam,* the pastoral region [16].

Of these five, *kuṟiñci* is clandestine, before marriage; *marutam* occurs after marriage. The other three could be either before or after marriage. *Pālai,* separation, includes not only the hardships of the lover away from his girl, but also the elopement of the couple, their hardships on the way and their separation from their parents. "Now, each landscape has its native elements (*karu*): gods, foods, animals, trees, birds, drums, occupations, lutes or musical styles and such others [20]." Flowers and kinds of running or standing water are also added.

Thus each phase of love gets its characteristic type of imagery from a particular landscape. Flower names like *kuṟiñci, mullai,* etc., are names not only of the landscape but of the associated feeling and of the type of poetry devoted to them.

Each of these landscapes is now a whole repertoire of images—anything in it, bird or drum, tribal name or dance, may be used to symbolize and evoke a specific feeling.

*Some Features of the Five Landscapes**

	LOVERS' UNION	PATIENT WAITING, DOMESTICITY	LOVER'S UNFAITHFULNESS, "SULKING SCENES"	ANXIETY IN LOVE, SEPARATION	ELOPEMENT, HARDSHIP, SEPARATION FROM LOVER OR PARENTS
Characteristic flower (name of region and poetic genre)	*kuṟiñci* (3)	*mullai* (jasmine) (234)	*marutam*	*neytal* (227)	*pālai* (an evergreen tree)
Landscape	mountains (3)	forest, pasture (220)	countryside (8)	seashore (123)	wasteland (mountain or forest parched by summer) (378)
Time	night (6, 153)	late evening (234)	morning	nightfall (226)	midday (378)
Season	cold season early frost (68)	rainy season (66)	all seasons	all seasons	late frost summer (378)
Bird	peacock (138) parrot (142)	sparrow, jungle hen (68)	stork, heron (25)	seagull	dove, eagle
Beast (including fish, reptile, etc.)	monkey (385) elephant (142) horse (74) bull (385)	deer (68)	buffalo freshwater fish (8)	crocodile (324) shark (269)	fatigued elephant, tiger, or wolf (56) lizard (16)
Tree or plant	jackfruit (18) bamboo (385) *vēṅkai* (47)	*koṉṟai* (66)	mango (8)	*aṭumpu* (243) *puṉṉai* (123)	*ōmai* (124) cactus (67)
Water	waterfall (95)	rivers (75)	pool (8)	wells (224) sea (226)	waterless wells, stagnant water (56)
Occupation and people	hill tribes (95) guarding millet harvest (142) gathering honey (3)	ploughman (131)	pastoral occupations (8)	selling fish and salt (269) fisherfolk (123)	wayfarers (124) bandits (12, 16)

* This is not an exhaustive list; only a few of the elements which appear frequently in the poems are given here. The names of gods, clans, musical instruments, and kinds of food have been omitted. The numbers refer to some of the poems which contain the particular images. Every poem in the anthology may be classified under one of the five types. See p. 108 for possible fusion of types, and the footnote about poem 68 on the same page.

A conventional design thus provides a live vocabulary of symbols; the actual objective landscapes of Tamil country become the interior landscape of Tamil poetry. A chart on page 107 tabulates some of these features. It would be useful to refer to the table of symbols when reading the poems.

The *Tolkāppiyam* takes care to add that "birds and beasts of one landscape may sometimes appear in others";* artful poets may work with a "confusion of genres" *(ṯiṇaimayakkam),* they may even bring in *puṟam* imagery to heighten the effects of an *akam* poem. He says: "the above genres are not rigidly separated; the time and place appropriate to one genre may be fused with the time and place appropriate to another. Anything other than *uri* or the appropriate mood may be fused or transformed. [19]"

For poetry the hierarchy of components is inverted; the Human Elements *(uri),* the Native Elements *(karu),* and the First Elements *(mutal)* are in a descending order of importance for a poet. Mere nature-description or "imagism" in poetry would be uninteresting to Tamil poets and critics.

Poetic Design

The conventions make for many kinds of economy in poetic design. Consider the very first poem of the selection:

What She Said

Bigger than earth, certainly,
higher than the sky,
more unfathomable than the waters
is this love for this man

* Poem 68 is a good example of this mixture of images. The season is early frost (*kuṟiñci*), but the bird mentioned is a jungle hen (*mullai*), the beast is a deer (*mullai*). The mixture of *kuṟiñci* (lovers' union) and *mullai* (patient waiting) brings out effectively the exact nuance of the girl's mood, "mixing memory and desire."

of the mountain slopes
where bees make rich honey
from the flowers of the *kuṟiñci*
that has such black stalks.

The *kuṟiñci* flower and the mountain scene clearly mark
the poem as a *kuṟiñci* piece about lovers' union. The union
is not described or talked about; it is enacted by the inset
scene of the bees making honey from the flowers of the
kuṟiñci. The lover is not only the lord of the mountain, he
is *like* the mountain he owns. Describing the scene de-
scribes his passion. The *kuṟiñci,* a tree that takes twelve
years to come to flower, carries a suggestion of the young
heroine who speaks the poem. The *Tolkāppiyam* calls this
technique of using the scene to describe act or agent *uḷḷuṟai*
("the inner substance").

The poem opens with large abstractions about her love:
her love is bigger than earth and higher than the sky. But
it moves toward the concreteness of the black-stalked
kuṟiñci, acting out by analogue the virgin's progress from
abstraction to experience.* We may remind ourselves that
this progression (from the basic cosmic elements to the
specific component of a landscape) is also the method of
the entire intellectual framework behind the poetry.

Further, in choosing earth, sky, and water for compari-
son, she has also chosen the constants of nature that make
up any particular scene. These constants, however, are con-
stantly interacting (cf. other poems like 40), mingling,
changing their states and forms. By implication her love,
which is constant through change, is greater than these
primal constants.

Evocations designed like these** may be seen in poem
after poem. "Inscapes" or *uḷḷuṟai's* of the natural scene

* For a very different effect from a similar focusing technique,
see poem 130.
** Other striking examples are 18, 25, 42, 68, 227, 243, 385.

repeat the total action of the poem. Note the irony of poem 8:

What the Concubine Said

You know he comes from
where the fresh-water shark in the pools
catch with their mouths
the mangoes as they fall, ripe
from the trees on the edge of the field.

At our place,
he talked big.

Now, back in his own,
when others raise their hands
and feet,
he will raise his too:

like a doll
in the mirror
he will shadow
every last wish
of his son's dear mother.

This is a *marutam* poem, a poem about infidelity; the shark, the pool at the edge of the meadow, and the mango are properties of the *marutam* landscape and define the *marutam* mood of ironic and sullen comment on a lover's infidelity. The poem moves from the openness of the fields to the closed indoors of the boudoir. The lover, by *uḷḷuṟai,* is the shark in the pool he owns; the fish gets all it wants without any effort. By comparing herself with the mango, the concubine is reproaching herself for being easily accessible. The last line also contrasts his carefree cavalier treatment of her with the tight-knit family in which he is now hemmed. Poem 67 uses imagery with a different effect:

What She Said

Will he remember, friend?
Where the curve of the parrot's beak
holds a bright-lit neem

like the sharp glory
of a goldsmith's nail
threading a coin of gold
for a new jewel,

he went across the black soil
and the cactus desert.

Will he remember?

The goldsmith's nail is the metaphor for a parrot's beak, the metaphor knitting the festive preparations of civilization with the fruition of nature. The brilliant colors of the body of the poem are drained to the bleakness of the cactus desert (evoking the *pālai* desert, and separation) by the end of the poem.

In natural languages, there are words that pass judgments on words ("that's a *beautiful* phrase," "it's an *ugly* word"); similarly there are poems dealing with the conventions themselves. Poem 226 is one.

What She Said

Before I laughed with him
nightly,

the slow waves beating
on his wide shores
and the palmyra
bringing forth heron-like flowers
near the waters,

my eyes were like the lotus
my arms had the grace of the bamboo
my forehead was mistaken for the moon.

But now

The speaker takes issue with the hackneyed phrases—"eyes like the lotus," "forehead like the moon"—and says, in effect, that such phrases are fine only when one is happy in love. Similarly, *Kuṟ* 234 takes up the conventional trappings of a *mullai* poem, which requires evening for its time, and confronts them with the real experience of lonely despair. Again and again, these poems cock an ironic self-critical eye at the writers' favorite strategies. These poems reflect upon poems; they are as much about love as about the nature of convention and poetic speech. A poem from *Naṟṟiṇai,* an *akam* anthology, expresses the cancellation of all abstract virtues and decorum (in poetry as in life) by one real experience:

What He Said

I had, as you'd wish,
courtesy
friendship
honor
usefulness
culture
and a considerate way
with others,

I had them all
before I set eyes
on the cold rich eyes
of this woman.

Naṟṟiṇai 160

The Personae

Little need be said about the characters or the situations which these poems imply. The dramatis personae are limited by convention to a small number: the hero, the heroine, the hero's friend(s) or messengers, the heroine's friend and foster-mother, the concubine, and passers-by. No poet here speaks in his own voice, and no poem is addressed to a reader. The reader only overhears what the characters say to each other, to themselves, or to the moon. A poem in this tradition implies, evokes, enacts a drama in a monologue.

The situations, when exactly a hero or heroine or one of their companions may speak out, and to whom, are also closely defined. For example,

> The girl-friend of the heroine may speak out on the following occasions: when the heroine, left behind by her lover, speaks of her loneliness; when she [the girl-friend] helps them elope; when she begs the hero to take good care of the heroine; when she tries to dissuade the parents from their search for the runaway couple, or to console the grieving mother . . . . [42].

Examples for these occasions may be found in poems like 16, 18, 42, 61.

The Episodes

If a reader cares to do so, he may arrange the situations in the poems in a certain narrative sequence, as the Tamil commentators tend to do. The narrative tends to illustrate the five phases: meeting (40), anxiety before marriage (25) and the symptoms of love (3, 6), the elopement (7) and probably the marriage (15), the lover's unfaithfulness and reconciliation (8), the going away of the lover, usually in search of wealth or conquest or knowledge, the pining and anxiety of the wife or beloved (11), as well as the hardships of the lover in the desert and his return (75). There are minor situations that stem from these: the girl-friend* asking the lover not to put off the day of marriage (18), her gentle reproach of the man's impatience to get to his girl (42), her anxiety for the hero and heroine (47)

* In several of the poems spoken by the girl-friend, she uses the collective "will he not really think of us?" or speaks of "our man" (514), "our love" (42). Some Western readers have found this strange; the implication is that the girl-friend is close enough to the heroine to feel a sense of identity. No polygamous arrangements are to be suspected.

or their disappointment at missing a tryst (244), the despair of the lover when his love threatens to remain unfulfilled (17), the heroine despairing of her man's return (46) and the friend's consoling words (66), the gossip of the town (24), and so on. For the most part, the situations are recreated by the poems themselves and need no annotation.

An interesting convention restricts the imagery for different speakers within the poems. The heroine's images are confined to what surrounds her house or to general notions and hearsay (3). Her girl-friend or foster-mother (324) has more ranging images: they are of a lower class, their experience is wider. The man's imagery has great range. Apparently there are no limits to his experience, and therefore to his imagery (56, 119). The range of imagery, not only its quality or content but also its very narrowness or width of choice, indirectly characterizes the speaker and his class.

The Two Proprieties

The *Tolkāppiyam* speaks of "two kinds of proprieties: those of Drama and those of the World." The conventional proprieties outlined so far are of the mode of drama. The situations of real life in the real world are governed by another set of proprieties. The strategy of the poet is to deploy both, to keep the tension between the forms of art and the forms of the world.

In a sense, the tradition of conventions does everything possible to depersonalize the poetry of *akam.* It gives all that can be *given* to a poet and makes of poetry a kind of second language.

The poet's language is not only Tamil; the landscapes, the personae, the appropriate moods, all become a language within language. Like a native speaker, he makes "infinite use of finite means," to say with familiar words what has never been said before; he can say exactly what he wants to, without even being aware of the ground-rules of his grammar. If the world is the vocabulary of the poet, the conventions are his syntax.

The Achievement of Caṅkam Poetry

The lyric poet likes to find ways of saying many things while saying one thing; he would like to suggest an entire astronomy by his specks and flashes. Toward this end, the Tamil poets used a set of five landscapes and formalized the world into a symbolism. By a remarkable consensus, they all spoke this common language of symbols for some five or six generations. Each could make his own poem and by doing so allude to every other poem which had been, was being, or would be written in this symbolic language. Thus poem became relevant to poem, as if they were all written by a single hand. The spurious name *Caṅkam* (fraternity, community) for this poetry is justified not by history but by the poetic practice.

In their antiquity and in their contemporaneity, there is not much else in any Indian literature equal to these quiet and dramatic Tamil poems. In their values and stances, they represent a mature classical poetry: passion is balanced by courtesy, transparency by ironies and nuances of design, impersonality by vivid detail, leanness of line by richness of implication. These poems are not just the earliest evidence of the Tamil genius. The Tamils, in all their 2,000 years of literary effort, wrote nothing better.

INDEX

POETS, SPEAKERS, and FIRST LINES

(Numbers used are not page numbers; they refer to the *Kur̲* number used with each poem.)

INDEX OF POETS

Fifty-one poets are represented in this selection. Some of them have a single name, others have the name of their city or their favorite poetic theme prefixed to their names. Some are known by their metaphors. Such descriptive names are indicated by English translation. Sometimes, a poet's name comes down in two or three forms, one of them usually honorific; the *-ar, -ār* plural suffixes at the ends of names are honorific, e.g., Patuman*ār,* Kapil*ar.* Names like Aḷḷūr Naṉmullaiyār (32) also appear without the honorific as Aḷḷur Naṉmullai (157). The names are alphabetized according to the roman transliteration; prefixes like Aḷḷūr are included in the name, and not treated as first names. Place names are marked by a+. The notes summarize the little that is known about the life of the poets.

NAME	POEMS	NOTES
Aiyūr+ Muṭavaṉ	123	Aiyūr was a city of the *Cōḷa* Kings. *Muṭavaṉ* means "a cripple." According to tradition his patron gave him bullocks and a chariot to transport himself.
Aḷḷūr+ Naṉmullai(yār)	32, 67, 157, 68	
Añcil+āntai(yār)	294	
Aṇilāṭu Muṉṟilār	41	"The Poet of the Yard Where the Squirrel Plays."
Aṟici Naccāttaṉār	271	
Auvai(yār)	15, 28, 99	According to some scholars, the Auvaiyār of *Caṅkam* is the same as a much-discussed prolific, oft-quoted woman poet whose witty and gnomic verses have become proverbial in Tamil. But there

NAME	POEMS	NOTES
		seems to have been more than one Auvaiyār (mother, woman saint). The Auvaiyār of the gnomic verses appears to be a later writer than the one in the *Caṅkam* anthologies, who sang of many kings.
Ālaṅkuṭi+ Vaṅkaṉār	8	
Āllattūr+Kiṛār	112	
Ātimanti(yār)	31	A woman poet. According to legend and her own poetry, she is supposed to have redeemed by her virtue her husband who was swept away in a flood. She is praised by other poets.
Catti Nātaṉār	119	
Cempulappeyaṉīrār	40	"The Poet of the Red Earth and Pouring Rain."
Ciṟaikkuṭiy+Āntaiyār	56	
Kaccippēttu+ Naṉṉākaiyār	30	A woman poet.
Kallāṭaṉār	269	"The man from *Kallāṭam.*" He wrote a commentary on *Tolkāppiyam.*
Kaḷḷil+āttiraiyaṉ	293	A learned Brahmin poet.
Kalporu Ciṟunuraiyār	290	"The Poet of the Foam on the Rocks."
Kaṇṇaṉ(ār)	244	
Kapilar	18, 25, 42, 95, 142, 153, 288, 312	A Brahmin and a friend of kings. Widely represented in the anthologies, he has a hundred poems on *kuriñci* themes in another anthology. With Paranar, this versatile poet is one of the best poets of the *Caṅkam* period.
Kavaimakaṉ	324	"The Poet of the Twins"
Kayamaṉar	378	"The Poet of the Eye in the Pool" (an image in another poem).
Kiḷimaṇkalaṅkirār	152	A farmer.
Kōkkul+muṟṟaṉ	98	
Kōṟi+kkoṟṟaṉ	276	
Kōvatattan	66	
Kutavāyiṟ+ Kirattaṉ	281	

NAME	POEMS	NOTES
Kūvaṉ Maintaṉ(ār)	224	"The Poet of (the Cow in the) Well."
Māmalaṭaṉ	46	The Poet of the *Malāṭu* region of ancient Tamil country.
Māmūlaṉār	11	A brahmin sage, named after the Lord under the Mango Tree. As his poems mention the *Manrya* kings, he is often dated as early as the second century B. C. He favors *pālai* themes. His work contains many historical references and includeṣ a grammar.
Maturai+ Eṛuttāḷaṉ	223	
Cēntampūtaṉ	226	Probably a scribe (Eṛuttāḷaṉ) of royal decrees in court.
Maturai+Kaṭaiyattār	223	
Makan Veṇṇakaṉ	223	
Māyeṇṭaṉ	235	
Miḷaipperuṅkantaṉ	136, 234	
Nampi Kuṭṭuvan	243	A descendant of the *Cēra* dynasty.
Neṭuveṇṇilaviṉār	47	"The Poet of the Long White Moonlight."
Okkūr+ Mācātti(yār)	126, 220, 275	A woman poet.
Ōreruravaṉār	131	"The Poet of the Plowman with a Single Ox."
Ōtalāntai(yār)	12	Has a 100 poems on *Pālai* themes in another anthology.
Ōta Ñāṉi	227	"Great Scholar."
Pālaipāṭiya Peruṅkaṭuṅkō	16, 124	"The poet-prince who sang of *Palai* themes," represented in several anthologies.
Paraṉar	24, 36, 292	Like Kapilar, a versatile poet, widely represented in the anthologies. Paraṇar and Kapilar are considered the best poets of the *Caṅkam* anthologies. Both wrote on *akam* and *puṟam* as well as on religious themes. His poems provide important details on contemporary cities, kings, and events.
Patumaṉār	6	Probably a Jain poet.

NAME	POEMS	NOTES
Paṭumarattu+ Mōcikīraṉ(ār)	33, 75	
Pēreyiṉ+ Muṟuvalār	17	
Perumpatumaṉar	7	
Peruñcāttaṉ	263	
Tēvakulattār	3	"The Poet of the Temple."
Tumpicērkiraṉ	61	"*Kīraṉ* of the Wandering Bee."
Tūṅkalōri	295	
Uṟaiyūr+ Mutukoṟṟaṉ	221	A stonemason *(koṟṟan)*? One of the many poets whose signature includes Uṟaiyūr,* the great center of learning and commerce of the classical period.
Uruttiraṉ	274	
Varumulaiyāritti	17	
Veḷḷi Vītiyār	130	A woman poet who seems to have written of a personal search for a lost husband. Like Ātimanti, another woman poet, one of the few *Cànkam* poets who seem to have written directly of personal experiences in an impersonal tradition.
Veṇmaṇippūti	299	A woman poet.
Veṇputi	97	Though the name suggests a woman, this poet is identified as a man of the farmer caste.
Viṭṭakutiraiyār	74	"The Poet of the Unleashed Horse."

* According to the classical author of the *Periplus of the Erythrean Sea* (about A.D. 75), who calls it *Argaru,* all the pearls gathered on the coast were sent to this Tamil metropolis; there was also much traffic in muslins called *Argaritic,* "thin as the slough of a snake or a cloud of steam."

INDEX OF SPEAKERS

Of the 401 poems in the *Kurr̲untokai,* the first is an invocation and the rest are divided among seven speakers: the heroine, 177; her girl-friend, 142; the hero, 62; the foster-mother, 9; the concubines, 6; passers-by, 3; the hero's friend, 2.

INDEX OF FIRST LINES